PRAISE

"Ethereal. Hypnotic. Oracular."
AMIE MCCRACKEN, AUTHOR OF *EMOTIONLESS*

"Jessica Bell captures motherhood in our daydreams and in our kitchens. It dances on a celestial plane, but then knocks the reader back down to Earth in an instant, with word combos only natural poets can weave. It's highly universal, yet still lands in its own category of brilliance."
ELAINA BATTISTA-PARSONS, AUTHOR OF *ITALIAN BONES IN THE SNOW*

"Each compelling meditation on daily life as mother and son blends the earthy with the ethereal. From Virginia Woolf and a grumbly fridge to sea spray, yucca leaf shadows, and fairies, these poems deliver discovery and delight."
MELANIE FAITH, AUTHOR OF *FROM PROMISING TO PUBLISHED*

"Profound observations about relationships between people, nature, and life experiences which left me gasping with both amazement and recognition. Mystical, wise and original."
KAREN ALGHABBAN, WRITER

"In *A Tide Should Be Able to Rise Despite Its Moon* Jessica Bell has thoroughly explored the topography of parenthood. She describes each moment with a keen eye and an open ear; with passion and with gentle understanding. You read her poems and say: 'Yes, that's exactly what it's like.'"
ALAN HUMM, EDITOR OF *ONE HAND CLAPPING* MAGAZINE

ABOUT THE AUTHOR

Jessica Bell is a multi-award-winning author/poet and singer-songwriter who was born in Melbourne, Australia.

In addition to having published a memoir, five novels, four poetry collections, and numerous craft books on writing and publishing, she is also the Publisher of Vine Leaves Press, and a highly sought-after book cover designer.

She currently resides in Athens, Greece, with her partner and son, and a pile of dishes that still don't know how to wash themselves despite her consistently teaching by example.

For more information visit:
iamjessicabell.com

·

"I'm not worried," I said. "I'll just charm her into giving me free room and board for as long as I want to live there."

Katie giggled. "Good luck with that plan, Mister."

Thank you for reading this book. I hope you found it both interesting and enjoyable. Please take a few minutes to leave a review on Amazon.com, Barnesandnoble.com, Goodreads, BookBub, Facebook, or Instagram.

You can also leave a comment or ask a question at www.marklredmond.com or email me at markredmond53@gmail.com. Photos of you holding a copy of one of my books are always welcome.

Check the next page for a list of all my books. If you visit my website and join my posse, I'll email you updates on new books as they're published; and I'll share news about other things happening in my world. My posse is growing, but there's room for you!

A TIDE SHOULD BE ABLE TO RISE DESPITE ITS MOON

POEMS

JESSICA BELL

A Tide Should Be Able to Rise Despite Its Moon
Copyright © 2023 Jessica Bell

Cover design by Jessica Bell
Interior design by Amie McCracken

"A single metaphor can give birth to love."

Milan Kundera

Dear

L **I** **F** **E**
i s o t
v   r e
i   r
n   n
g   i
          t
          y

I hear you.

A breath of earth hides in shallow water.

A small boy disrupts its peace as he plucks it
from its bed of black sand
to use as a skipping stone.

It slips and glides across the bay—
an infinite shawl of purple silk
glimmering under the blood red moon.

Inside the stone lives the gentle touch of a little girl
who once protected the same soul
as the boy who threw it.

The stone licks the surface of the water
seven times before sinking back down
into its bed of a hundred years.

It lands next to a shell
that shimmers with the dreams
of the boy's mother and father.

They dreamed he would live in the colours
of a rainbow, and smile.

The boy looks up.

The clouds part.

His eyes grew wet
when we met on the couch for dinner.
It was a touching show.
Bringing home the joys and woes
of childhood.

We flicked through year-old photos
on my phone.

We remarked how much he'd grown—
And how fast.

We glanced at the measurements
on the wall
and exchanged smiles.

Bon appetite he said, and leaned in for a kiss.

Then we ate without turning on the TV.

He's only three.

I believed it was a *prison*
of light as a child.
Fairies clutched at glowing strings
screaming to be saved.

The *youth in Asia* also got
a lot of thought
whenever my parents argued
about the right to choose
life over death.

I never understood, either,
how *losing your religion*
could make you *pee*
in the corner.
I once peed in the corner of my bedroom
and all I lost was pee.

Spell father, said my prep teacher.
F A R T E R.

Twenty years later...
You'll never be a writer.

Well.

Red wine
slows the head and the hand.

I write like I imagine
Virginia Woolf would
with a fountain pen.

The only difference being
the ceramic nibbed pen
and e-ink device.

The only stain that remains
is in my mind.

My mind is blocked
with snot and mania.

100 books have *fallen*
off the bookshelf.

Frustration and anger
linger inside post nasal drip.

I swallow words
that should not be said.

He's just a child.

I go to the bathroom;
cough those words up as phlegm.
and flush my sickness
down the drain.

He's just a child.
But he needs to learn.

When I come out,
the books are sleeping
back in their shelves.

I stare at Daddy,
you shouldn't have done that.

But then I see,
the poet-tree.

A tall thin tree sits alone
in the park—
its trunk surrounded
by concrete and potting mix.

The wind blows.
Its branches bend toward
the other trees in the park—
the trees whose trunks
are rooted
into true earth.

The tall thin tree
tries to touch the others' leaves.
It hopes to understand
what it feels like
being connected to Mother.

But no matter how hard it tries
the foreign soil that nurtures its soul
still overpowers its desires.

The tall thin tree sits alone in the park,
its branches bend toward itself.

A faceless child
navigates the moist mossy rocks
on the bed
of our local creek.

A simple breeze
rustles leaves—
maracas of our earth.

The current tickles
brave and inquiring ankles;
the sound of trickling
devours our souls.

An onlooker stares.

The child removes the clothes
that mask our spirit
and immerses the truth
of our skin
in water.

The reflection of my face
appears before the fish.
Ripples distort my eyes.

These vehicles of my soul,
detach and dissipate,
momentarily emptying
my art and mind; momentarily
deeming vision
a prosthetic.

He stares through tinted glass
toward the sea.
The salty breeze
wafts through half-open vents.
He tries to roll
a cigarette
as the window eases open
with an electronic zing,
but the tobacco falls
between his toes.

He watches his son
as he dips his own toes
into the white foam
that licks the sand.

I will buy you a house by the sea, son.
One day, I will make it happen. I promise.

It's been over five years
since they spoke.

The road you walk is chiselled
yet it can be sailed on smoothly
in your romanticized perception
of your everyday.

The road you walk is chiselled
yet you stumble over boulders
in your tragic perception
of your everyday.

The road you walk is chiselled
yet you are oblivious to its pitfalls
in your impulsive perception
of your everyday.

The road you walk is chiselled
and you feel every bump
in the reality
of your everyday.

The road you walk is not chiselled
It is an ocean; a body.

It is not a road at all.
It is you.

The hum between the screen
and my face
scaffolds the last breath
of hope we have.

Two years of texts
were not enough
to hold together sixteen
years of us.

We were a constant
and now we're a sigh.

It spills from my lips
in drips, marking its
territory with grief stains
that do not respond to bleach.

How long should I hold on
in this mottled skin?

A tide should still be able to rise
despite its moon.

Rope may keep the boats in the bay,
but will we always have the choice
to untie them?

If only that rope
didn't also join our wrists
to our neighbors.

Escape
has become e-scape—
and endless digital horizon.
No gravity, no destination,
but lots of clouds
to float in.

We glitch through light—
a time warp of connection
forgetting our own tangible bodies
can actually escape on land
and thrive.

The steel ceiling
shudders below
my sweaty hot feet.

The sofa rattles against my back.

I sway left and right as children squeal
and mothers steal glances at the sky.

The sun sets behind a misty horizon.
The gangway thuds against a rocky pier.

See spray flicks my face
as the engines of trucks rumble.

I disembark—the smell
of familiarity shifts me back
thirty years.

It still doesn't feel like home.

But now I have a son.

The fridge
it does not hum.
It grumbles and squeaks.
And often leaks
complaints like air
seeping through a puncture in a balloon.

When it cries
like my little boy
waking from a nap,
I rise and bolt to his room
to find him fast asleep—
his smile stroking dreams.

And then
I do not think of the fridge at all.

It wasn't too long ago
when I heard the sound of a smile—
the way it eased across my son's face
and vibrated the room.

My camera cannot capture it.

Sometimes we see more
with our eyes closed.

Water screams down my head
my back, my legs—
my penis.

The touch of a goddess.

Laughter surrounds me
through hesitant mouths
Candles burn as love
collides with expectation,
and joy is transferred
from hand to hand.

I am cold and naked.
My toes drip into a bliss bowl.
I cry so loud,
it echoes beyond the church.

My trembling hands reach for the coffee pot.
A voice tells me to wait.
The mind will cool
as the vapor rises and sleeps
on the underside of the kitchen cupboards.
It will either drip or dry.
Depends on the temperature.

Thankfully,
the weather will always start
a conversation.

The truck beeps its horn
as a signal to the jeep
that it is approaching.

The jeep stops in the middle
of the busy four-lane highway
at a set of red traffic lights.

The jeep opens the door
for its driver.
The driver steps out—
face contorted like a gargoyle.
It yells,
What the fuck is your fuckin' problem?

The truck's engine rolls—
chilled in neutral.
Its driver steps out of the vehicle—
smirking like a cheeky child.

The rumble of the engine
is a backdrop for its forthcoming message.

Nice weather today, huh?

The jeep's driver stares—
and scoffs.

And then.
They shake hands.

Yucca leaf shadows
spread like fingers
across the balcony.

They yearn for sunshine
and stretch their limbs
toward the scorching light.

A red plastic spade sleeps
in a pit of potting mix.
It's half-melted handle
reaches toward the yucca shadows,
creating a shadow of its own.

In summer the balcony drowns in shadows,
but not human ones.
In winter it longs to be stroked again,
with their feather-like souls.

Sometimes,
I try to cast mine.

But the trees seem confused,
and the dragon flowers hide.

Humans and nature
are not great collaborators.

Today the cicada's call
is a communal *tsk* at the world.
I sit on a mountaintop
staring at the blue deep below,
and an incomprehensible horizon
whose line is too faint to follow.

As I try to find an opening
between earth and sky,
they shake their hands at me
in surround sound.

The engine of a moped
accents their disapproval;
I record their voices in ink—
the size of my letters
decrease on each line.

They hush and shush me
to a written whisper.
We're not asking, we're telling.
I've heard this message before.

I am not the first to listen
and not know where to go
from here.

Words float across the lake
and stroke the edges of row boats
hidden inside ripples of water.

They spit their woes
and dampen floors
with all the misdemeanours
of a holiday crowd.

Eleftheria's anchor is lifted
and with the push of two oars
she paints the bay with gossip.

Thunder cracks and rain
mixes words with clouds.

Some thoughts are drowned
others are evaporated
into breaths of hate.

Dreams are inhaled by hosts
who do not deserve them.

Dry opinions are mixed
with wet opinions
and vomited from poisoned minds.

The lake turns red and the sky black.

I wait for years to see another star.

I pace.
The decking creaks.
My dirty boots spill illusions.
Renovation instructions muffle,
reverberate the hot phone against my ear.
I will not hear another word.
Not about the yellow blow-up duck pool.

They'll have to work around the last place
his tiny soft feet splashed.

My son
runs circles around us.
On paper
he perceives his life
in wheels, balls, moons,
suns, and planets.
His eyes roll
when we praise
his ability to draw.
He's been places
in his 2D cars
many lifetimes over.
When he dies
he'll become the earth.
The circle of life
is inside him.
Or should I say,
around him.

Carry me, he says
chewing on a piece of raw potato
as I cut vegetables to roast.

I'm cooking.
You're watching.
You're nibbling.
Don't you like it?

He lifts his arms to reignite his request.

Why?

Because I love you.

He's learned the art
at three.

As he reaches for my breast
in the middle of the night
I watch his mouth bite
off my nipple.

He then chews on my fingers
like chicken wings
snaps off my toes
smacks his lips—
his desperate moan a signal
of delight.

His tummy now full,
he strokes my arm
and wipes my freckles off.
As he runs his fingers through his hair
it turns to worms.

His nose bleeds as he smiles
and bares his tiny white teeth,
embedded in gums
infected with comfort.

Little black bugs emerge
from between his gaps
and crawl into his eyes.

He is blind.

But I will never stop seeing.

My 22-year-old
electric guitar
leans against my bed
room wall
I see it every morning
when I open my eyes.

My 15-year-old
acoustic guitar
leans against the electric guitar—
protecting it from
my urges to play
that end in disappointment,
self-disgust,
and the woman below
banging a broom
on her ceiling.

My 3-year-old
son ties
my dressing gown's
belt around
the acoustic neck,
drags it around the house
along the floor
pretending to have caught
a sea beast.

What he actually catches
is my heart from my throat.

The strings have not felt
the massage of my fingertips
until now—
through the mesh
of a microfibre cloth.

His green eyes glimmer
through a look of concern.
No, stop, stop!
Play with me, mummy.

Yes, mummy. *Play.*
Why don't you?

I look into my lap
and I'm destroyed by the view
of stomach flab covering my groin.
How, when, *how, when?*
I can't even write,
make music, cook, watch TV ...
sleep.

The wardrobe mirrors
reflect water mattress thighs.
I weigh myself naked.
63.7. I lost one!
I weigh myself again to be sure.
64.8? You temperamental piece of shit
from I Know Everything About you!

Weight has become the vocalist of every band,
the author of every book,
the reason behind why I will fail
at everything
until it is lost.

I postpone my exercise plan
another day
for when I can no longer do
up the last button.
I slouch on the couch—
stuff my face
with peanut butter sandwiches.

My son sits at my feet,
on the floor.
It's hot, and he's naked.
He pushes his tummy
in and out, in and out.
He giggles.

Mummy, look!

I'm already looking.
And now, I smile.

How long does it take
to buy onions
from the corner store?

As long as it takes
to consider buying
everything you don't need.

How long does it take
to put your shoes on?

As long as it takes
to find the other shoe.

How long does it take
to find the red Cadillac
with George stuck on the roof
with Blu Tack
when your son won't stop crying
until it's found?

Forever.

How long does it take
to live in the moment?

One second.

What are we afraid of
when we say no.
What compromise are we making
when we say yes.
What are we hiding
when we say maybe.
What are we avoiding
when we don't socialize.
What are we escaping
when we are distracted.
What are we making
when we put the kettle on?

English Breakfast.

Leeches suck the marrow
from my mind
and deposit it in the ground.

From the ground
grows a brain.

This brain is quiet.
Pure.

Until someone digs it up
and throws it
to their dog.

The dog, it chews;
its flavor familiar.
It barks for more,
but there is none.

My brain is gone.
But my mind—
it will ignite again.

Triangular redless faces caress the yellowness of the bricks that house the little pig that lost the little brother too and the big bad howlin' wolf that doesn't roar and doesn't soar across the forest filled with bees and little blond boys and toys and hamster wheels, moaning seals and orange peels, desires and tears that make you vomit all the moons and stars and comets through the mouth of your red soul.

Breath.

Reignition complete.

I feel power
when bitten
by Obsidian.

My son walks
on lava
and saves me from falling in
by sitting on my lap.

My son was birthed
by volcanic rock,
where everything is possible
and every danger, safe.

I have burned,
and I will continue to burn,
so that fire stands for beauty,
not fear.

And when we die,
cremation will bring us home.

And life will start again.

Why is there no unclichéd way
to describe the sea
glistening under the sun?
When I stand on the shore
And let the waves lick my feet;
when I watch the birds fly
in front of a sun set;
when the leaves swish in the breeze
and send my soul soaring above it all?

Why is it clichéd to admire the sea
and how it glistens under the sun?

Human eyes
and minds.

Plastic pliers lie
between green plasticine
and Jessie the Jeep.

A half-drunk cup
of almond milk
warms by Frank the Fire Truck.

Its ladder is lost
in the abyss of our coffee
table slash treasure chest
from I Know Everything About you,
built with criss-crossed wood
creepers would die for.

Before he went to sleep
the plastic pliers hit my son,
and he said,
I want to take my head
and throw it on the floor.

There are spaces between
the do this, do thats
and insects under the bed.

There are no such things
as monsters, *don't be silly.*

Worms, there are worms
lots of little worms
that crawl in your nose
and out your ears
in the middle of the night
and around your nipples, mummy.

Wipe my snot,
fix my hair,
I want boobie in the backseat.

Close your eyes,
find a space,
you can breathe in there.

Shall I sing you song?
Yes.

There's lots of space
in a song.

The soft hum of the engine
sterilizes the darkness of silence
in the back seat.
The weight of my child
in my lap—a comfort.
I wrap my arms around his waist
and rest my lips on the crown of his head.
He turns to face the window,
pressing his cheek
to my breast.
His baby smell a memory.
Or perhaps ... not just yet.

In the speckled darkness
of a city night,
you're oh so quiet,
in the back seat.
Are you okay?

Lights flash over your face
as we drive…
as we drive—
and your eyes, they are glazed
are you sick?
are those tears?
is there something you don't understand?

Should I ask,
or do I let you zone out,
to piece together the workings
of the world,
you somehow know better than me.

You're oh so quiet.

Are you okay?

Yes, I'm okay.
I have bones in my body,
and blood in my body.
Of course, I'm okay.

Life is simple.
It's easy to forget.

An empty wine glass sits
between a puzzle of vintage cars
and the story of Mr Sneeze.

Mummy smokes a cigarette—
imaginary.

A little boy sleeps
in the next room—
real.

It will all happen again
tomorrow.

Or perhaps,
it won't.

The gift from Madoc, with help from his dad, after the bookshelf incident.

ACKNOWLEDGEMENTS

One day, when there were workers banging somewhere in our apartment building, I drew my son's attention to the noise. He had just turned two. I said, "Listen. Can you hear it? What's that noise?" My son replied, "It's heartbeat of building."

Since then, he has been an endless well of inspiration.

This is the first book of poems I've published in almost ten years. It exists because of him. My son.

Madoc Maximus Karmios-Bell, thank you.

MORE POETRY
FROM THE AUTHOR

Muted & She
Fabric
Twisted Velvet Chains

VINE LEAVES PRESS

Enjoyed this book?
Go to *vineleavespress.com* to find more.
Subscribe to our newsletter:

Lightning Source UK Ltd.
Milton Keynes UK
UKHW012318070223
416638UK00004B/47

9 783988 320940